GRAPHIC LIBRARY™

GRAPHIC SCIENCE

ADVENTURES IN SOUND

WITH **MAX AXIOM**
SUPER SCIENTIST

by Emily Sohn

illustrated by Cynthia Martin
and Anne Timmons

Consultant:
Dr. Ronald Browne
Associate Professor of Elementary Education
Minnesota State University, Mankato

Capstone
press

Mankato, Minnesota

Graphic Library is published by Capstone Press,
151 Good Counsel Drive, P.O. Box 669, Mankato, Minnesota 56002.
www.capstonepress.com

Printed in the United States of America

1 2 3 4 5 6 12 11 10 09 08 07

Library of Congress Cataloging-in-Publication Data
Sohn, Emily.
Adventures in sound with Max Axiom, super scientist / by Emily Sohn; illustrated by Cynthia Martin and Anne Timmons.
p. cm.—(Graphic library. Graphic science)
Summary: "In graphic novel format, follows the adventures of Max Axiom as he explains the science behind sound"—Provided by publisher.
Includes bibliographical references and index.
ISBN-13: 978-0-7368-6836-5 (hardcover)
ISBN-10: 0-7368-6836-4 (hardcover)
ISBN-13: 0-7368-7889-0 (softcover pbk.)
ISBN-10: 978-0-7368-7889-0 (softcover pbk.)
1. Sound—Juvenile literature. 2. Adventure stories—Juvenile literature. I. Martin, Cynthia, 1961– ill. II. Timmons, Anne, ill. III. Title. IV. Series.
QC225.5.S64 2007
534—dc22 2006027995

Art Director and Designer
Bob Lentz

Cover Artist
Tod Smith

Colorist
Michael Kelleher

Editor
Christopher L. Harbo

Photo illustration credits: Scott Thoms/Capstone Press, 8 (bottom)

TABLE OF CONTENTS

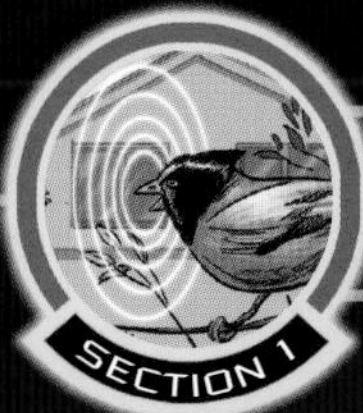
SECTION 1

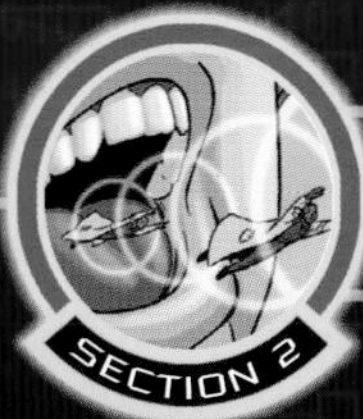
SECTION 2

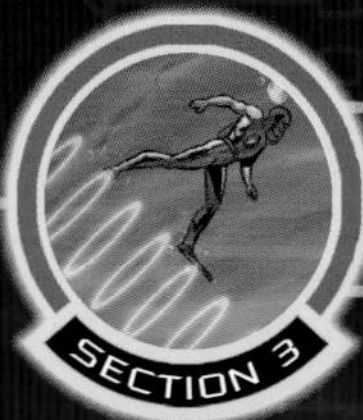
SECTION 3

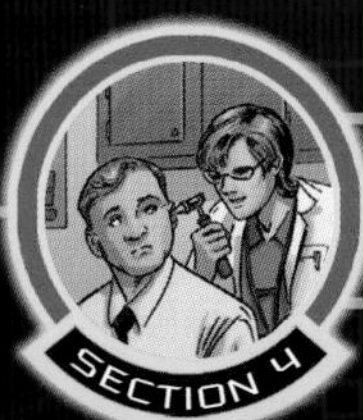
SECTION 4

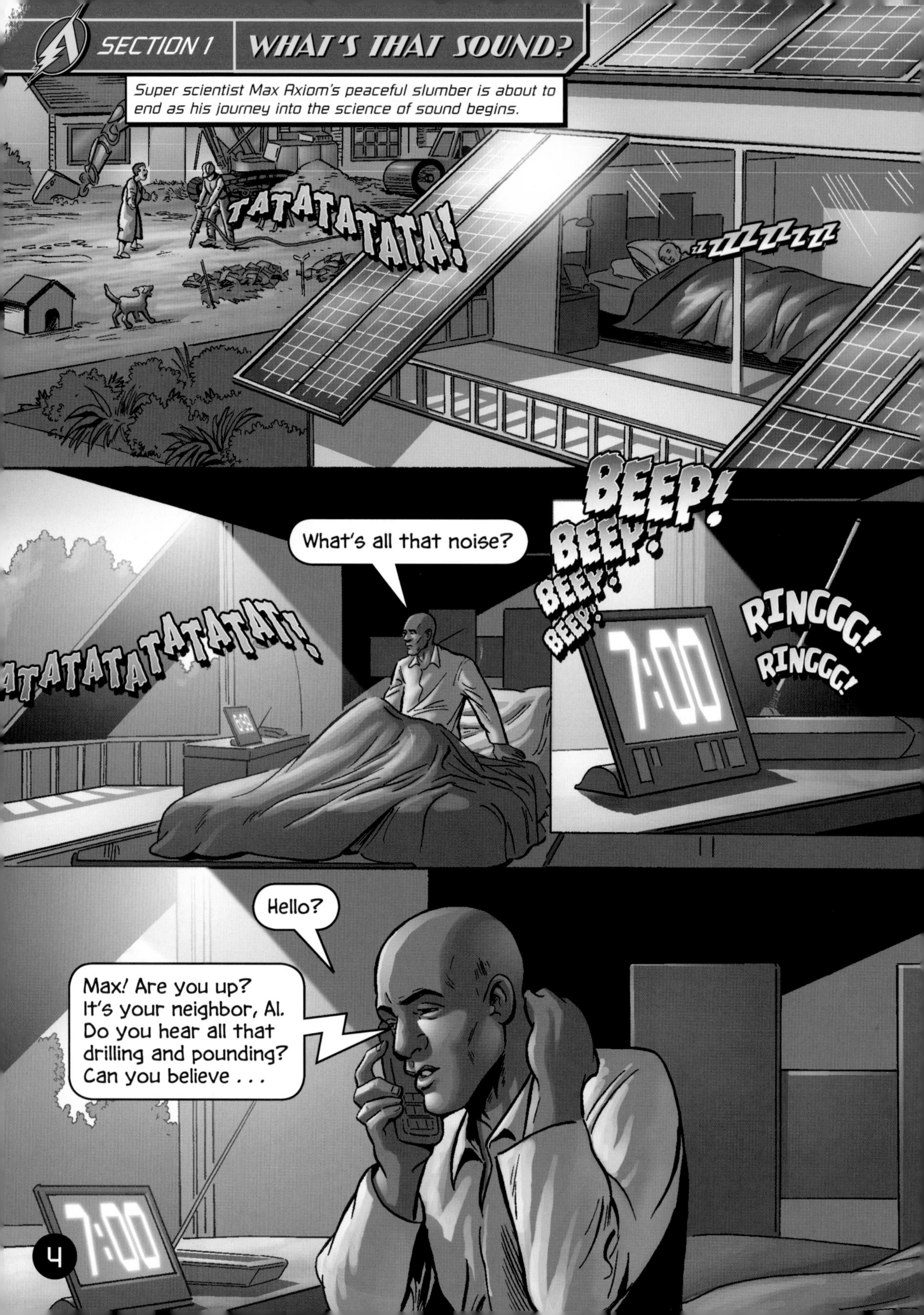
SECTION 1
WHAT'S THAT SOUND?
Super scientist Max Axiom's peaceful slumber is about to end as his journey into the science of sound begins.
TATATATATATA!
ZZZZZZZZ
What's all that noise?
TATATATATATATATAT!!
BEEP! BEEP! BEEP! BEEP!
7:00
RINGGG! RINGGG!
Hello?
Max! Are you up? It's your neighbor, Al. Do you hear all that drilling and pounding? Can you believe . . .
7:00

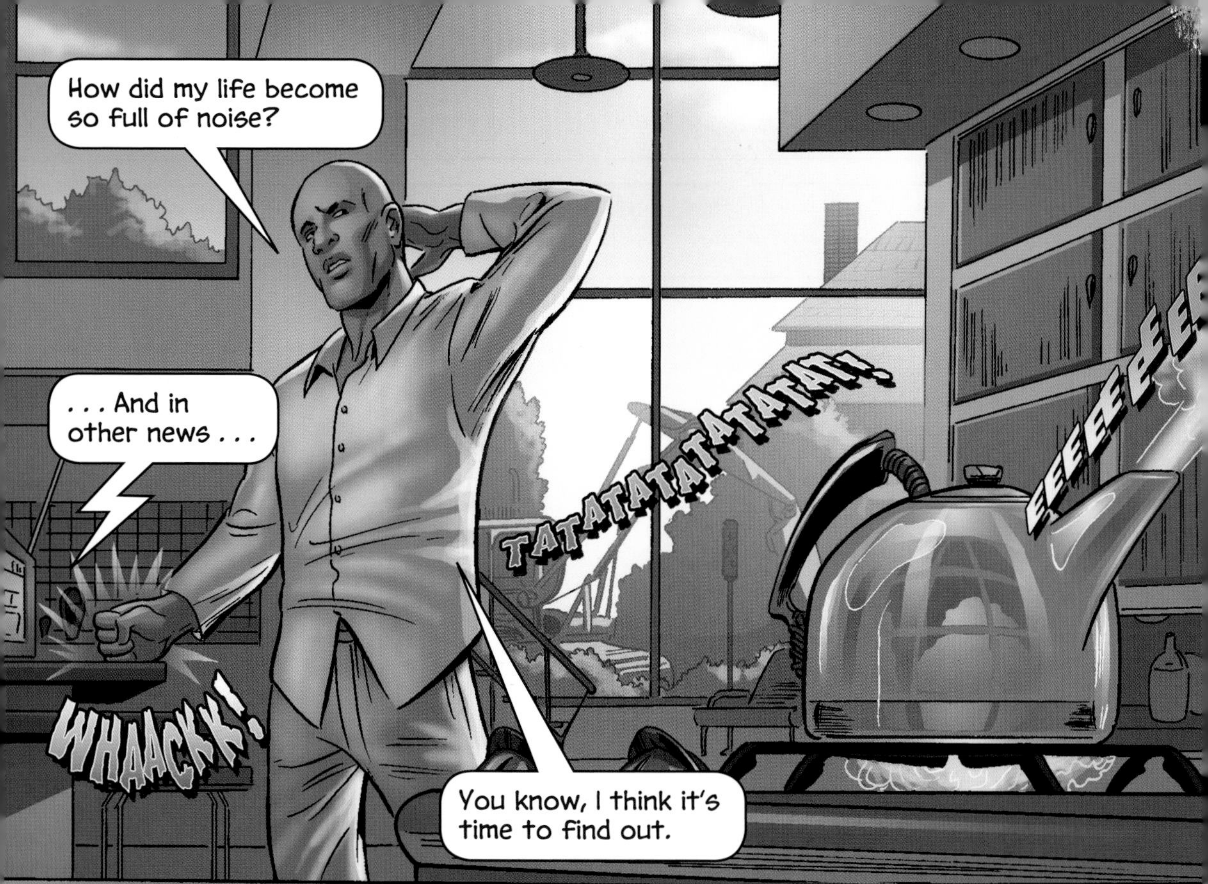
How did my life become so full of noise?
. . . And in other news . . .
WHAACKK!
TATATATATATATATAT!!
EEEEEEEEE
You know, I think it's time to find out.

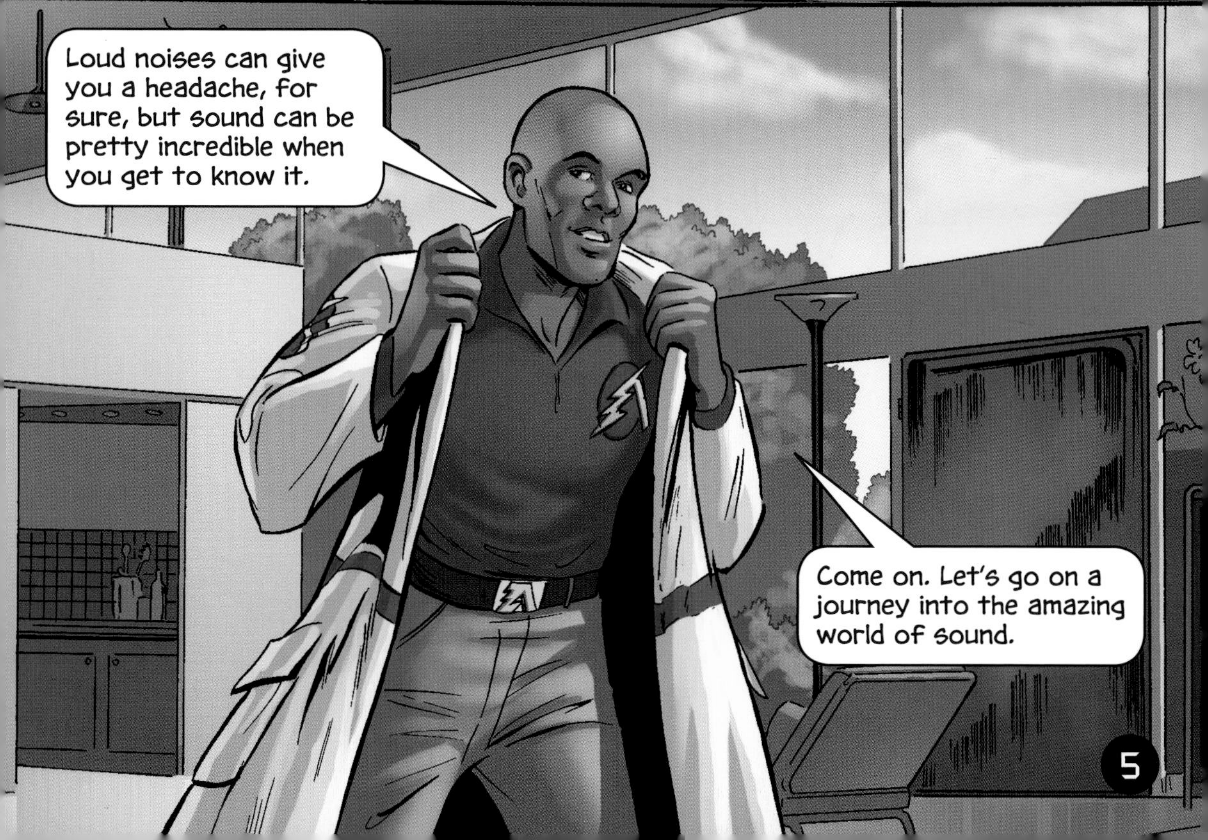
Loud noises can give you a headache, for sure, but sound can be pretty incredible when you get to know it.
Come on. Let's go on a journey into the amazing world of sound.

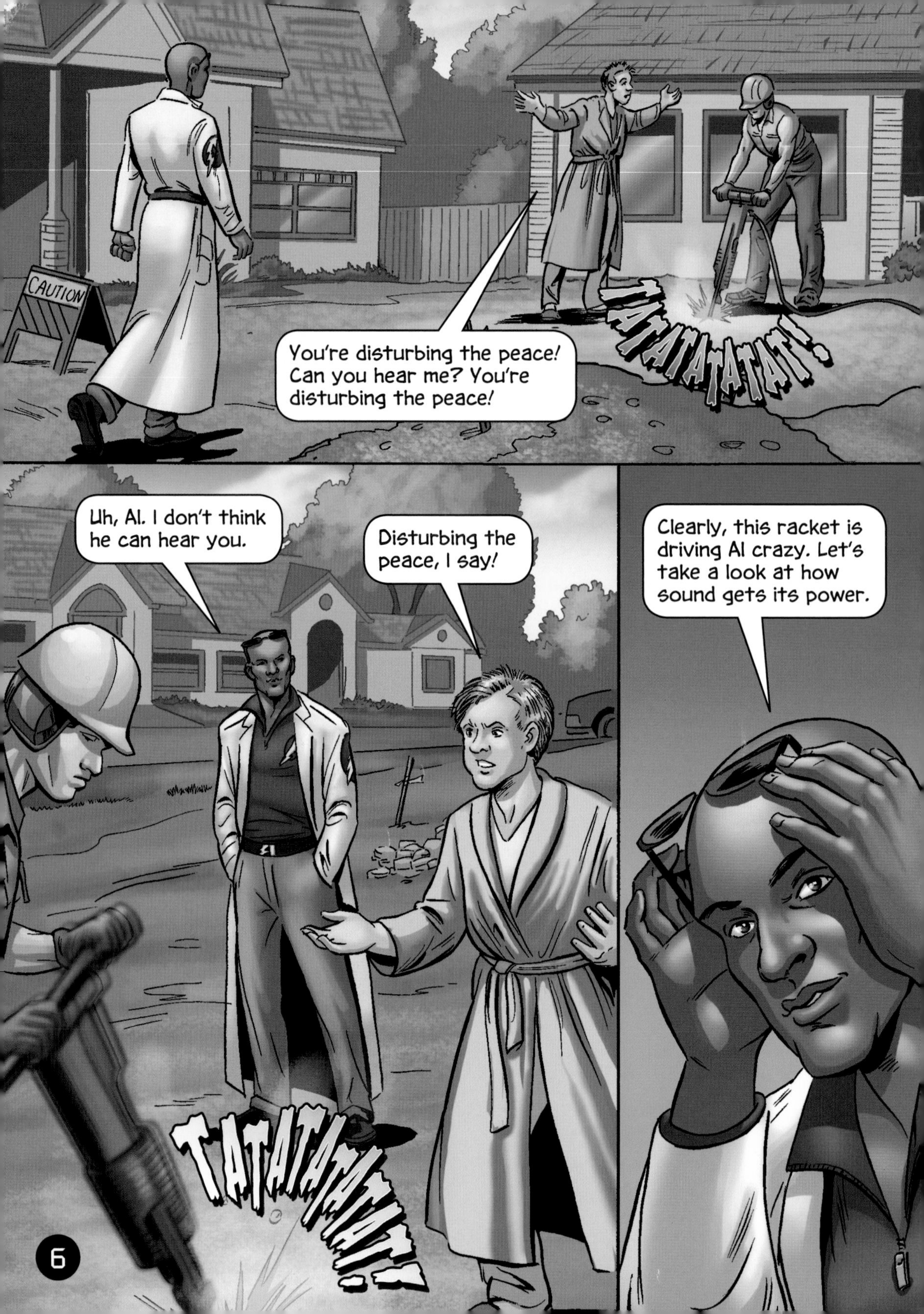
You're disturbing the peace! Can you hear me? You're disturbing the peace!
Uh, Al. I don't think he can hear you.
Disturbing the peace, I say!
Clearly, this racket is driving Al crazy. Let's take a look at how sound gets its power.

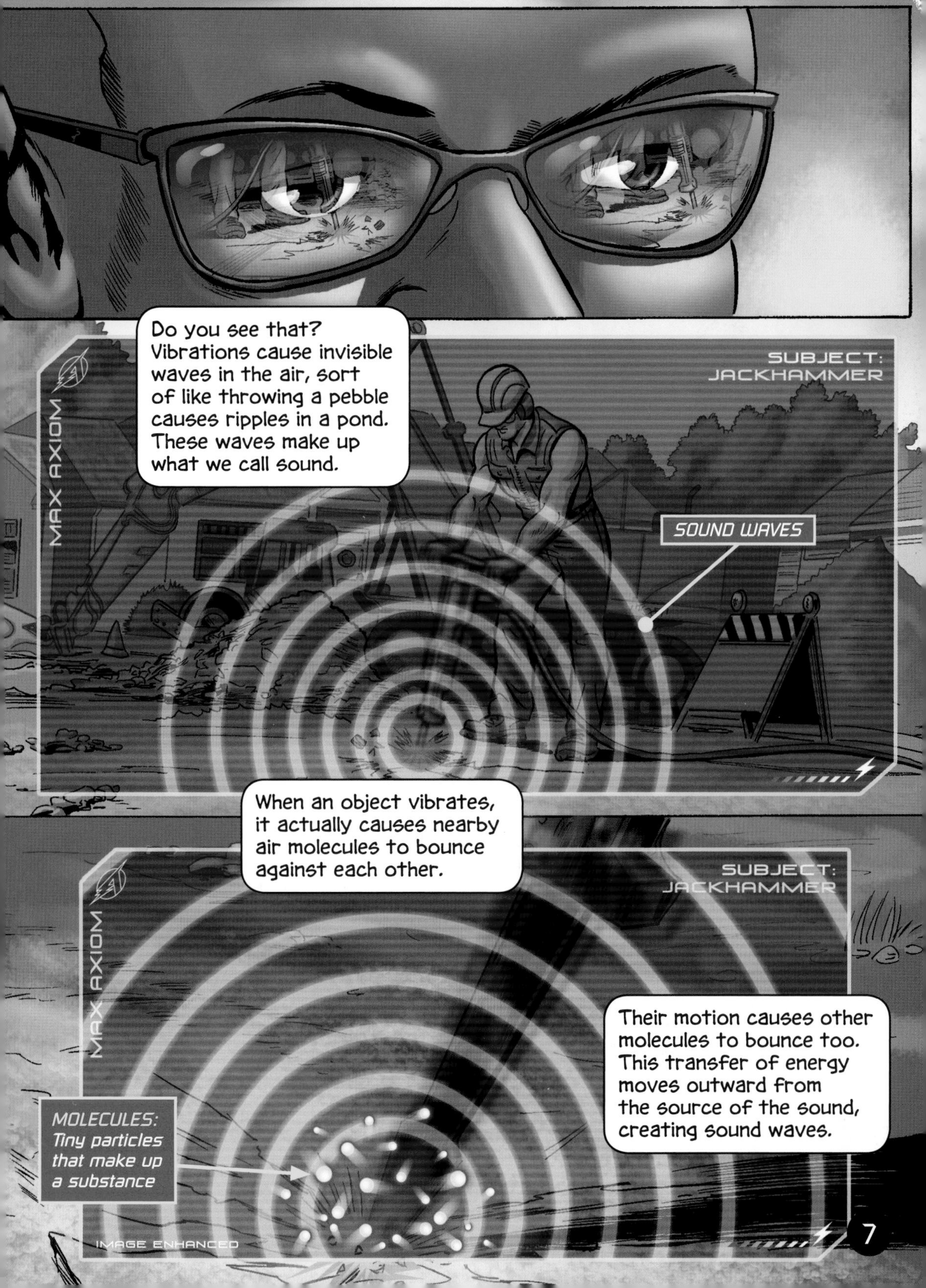

Do you see that? Vibrations cause invisible waves in the air, sort of like throwing a pebble causes ripples in a pond. These waves make up what we call sound.
MAX AXIOM
SUBJECT: JACKHAMMER
SOUND WAVES
When an object vibrates, it actually causes nearby air molecules to bounce against each other.
MAX AXIOM
SUBJECT: JACKHAMMER
Their motion causes other molecules to bounce too. This transfer of energy moves outward from the source of the sound, creating sound waves.
MOLECULES: Tiny particles that make up a substance
IMAGE ENHANCED

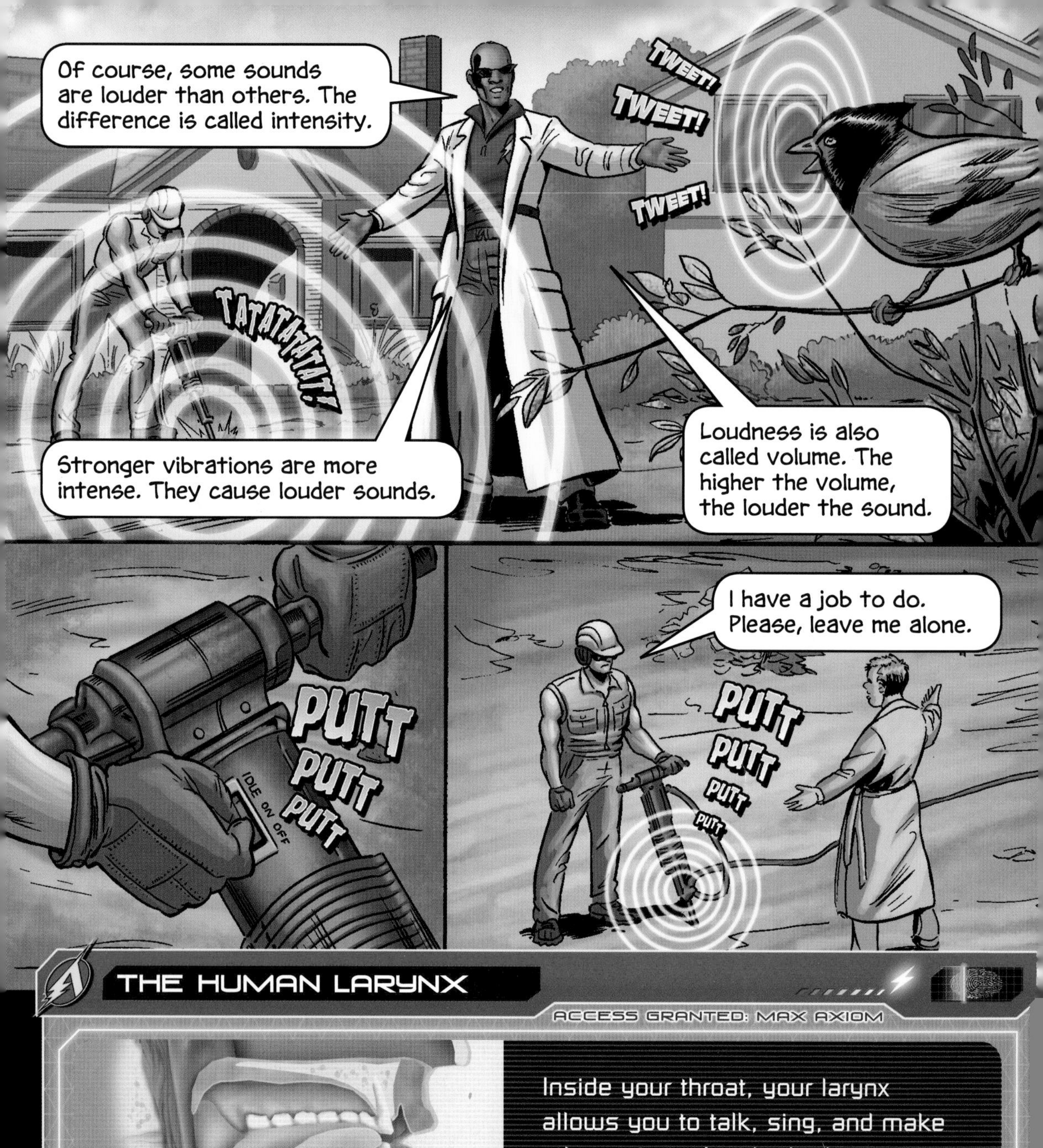
Of course, some sounds are louder than others. The difference is called intensity.
TWEET!
TWEET!
TWEET!
TATATATATATAT!
Stronger vibrations are more intense. They cause louder sounds.
Loudness is also called volume. The higher the volume, the louder the sound.
IDLE ON OFF
PUTT
PUTT
PUTT
I have a job to do. Please, leave me alone.
PUTT
PUTT
PUTT
PUTT

THE HUMAN LARYNX

ACCESS GRANTED: MAX AXIOM

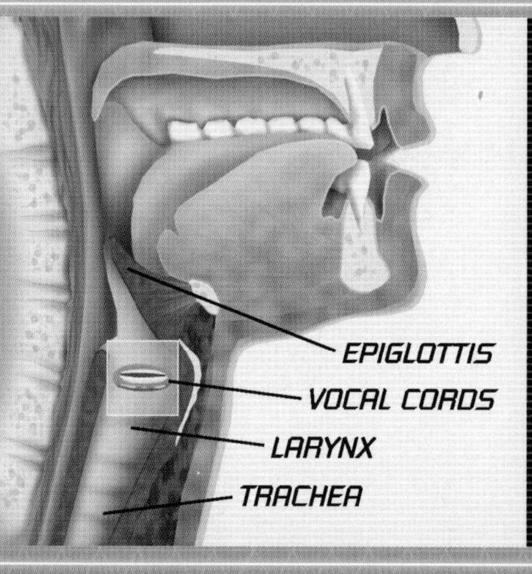
EPIGLOTTIS
VOCAL CORDS
LARYNX
TRACHEA

Inside your throat, your larynx allows you to talk, sing, and make other noises. Inside the larynx, two muscles called vocal cords squeeze together and vibrate as air passes by them. The faster they vibrate, the higher your voice sounds. Your tongue and lips shape the sounds you make.

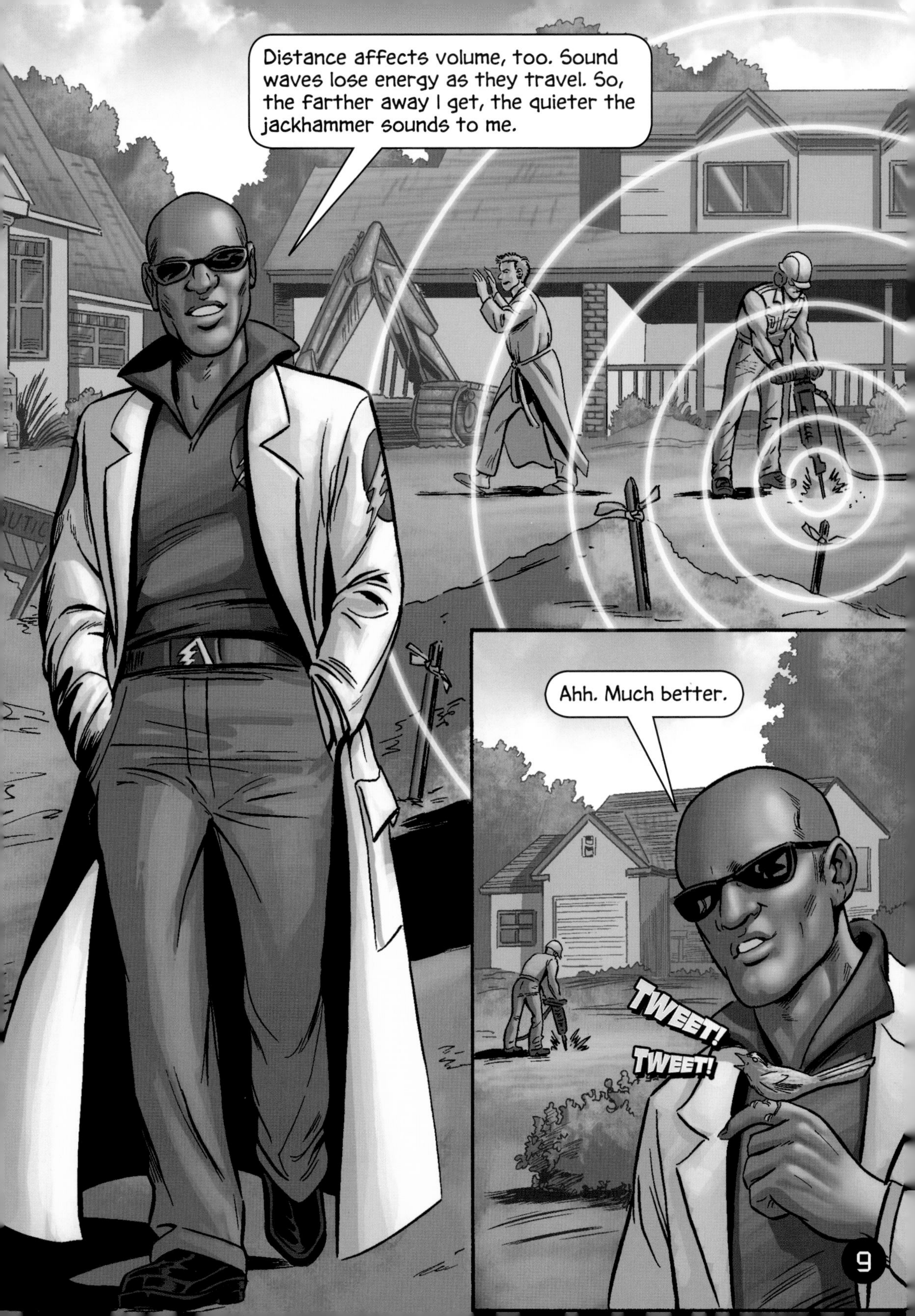
Distance affects volume, too. Sound waves lose energy as they travel. So, the farther away I get, the quieter the jackhammer sounds to me.
Ahh. Much better.
TWEET!
TWEET!

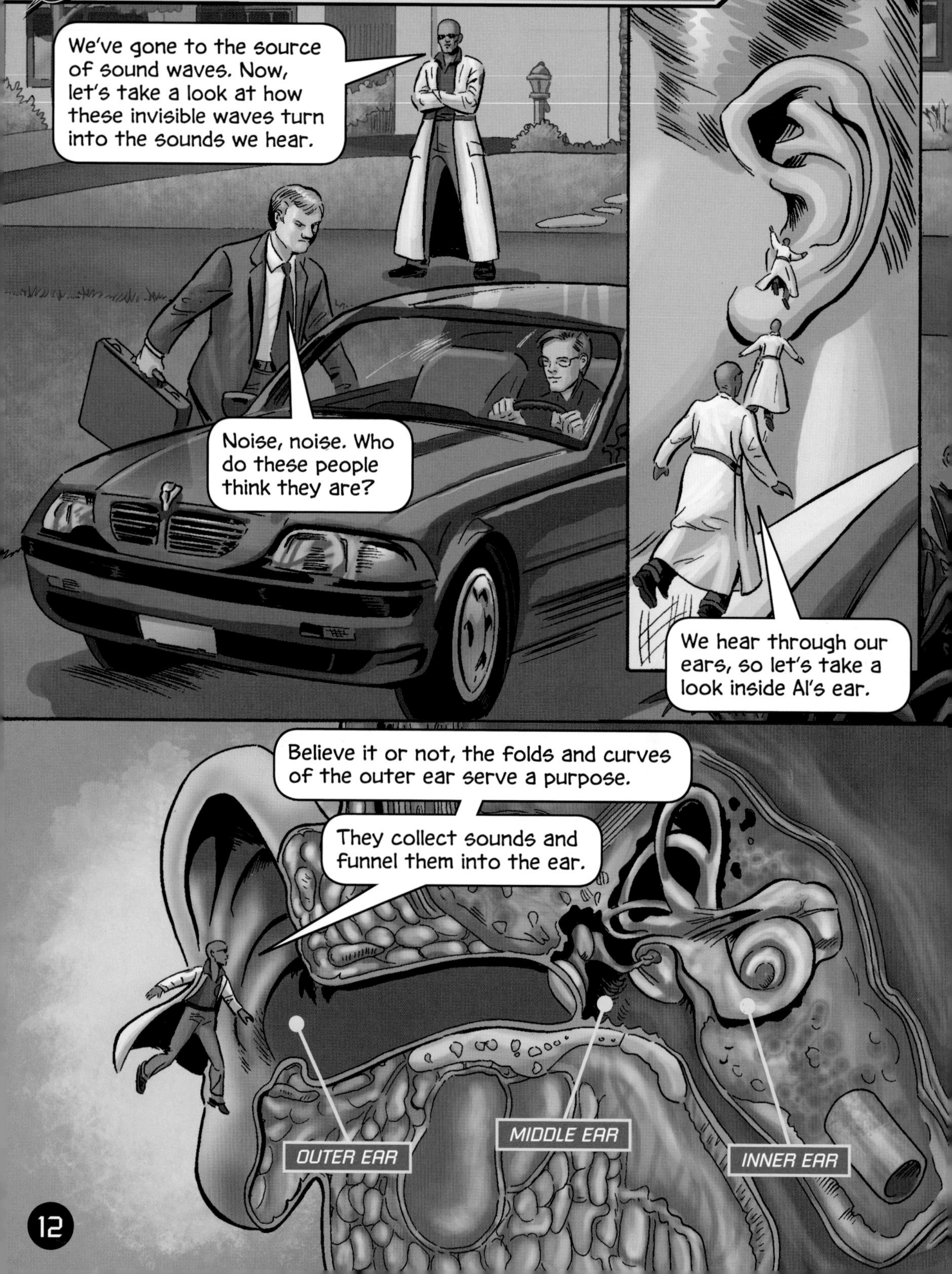

We've gone to the source of sound waves. Now, let's take a look at how these invisible waves turn into the sounds we hear.
Noise, noise. Who do these people think they are?
We hear through our ears, so let's take a look inside Al's ear.
Believe it or not, the folds and curves of the outer ear serve a purpose.
They collect sounds and funnel them into the ear.
OUTER EAR
MIDDLE EAR
INNER EAR

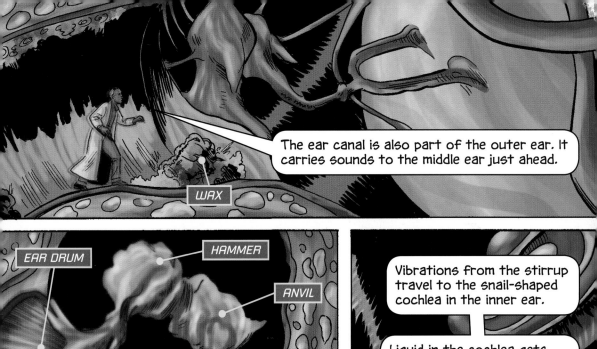

The ear canal is also part of the outer ear. It carries sounds to the middle ear just ahead.

WAX

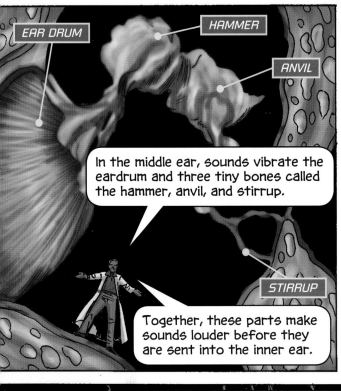

EAR DRUM

HAMMER

ANVIL

In the middle ear, sounds vibrate the eardrum and three tiny bones called the hammer, anvil, and stirrup.

STIRRUP

Together, these parts make sounds louder before they are sent into the inner ear.

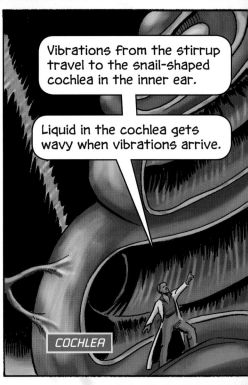

Vibrations from the stirrup travel to the snail-shaped cochlea in the inner ear.

Liquid in the cochlea gets wavy when vibrations arrive.

COCHLEA

These are hair cells inside the cochlea. They send electrical signals to the brain. The signals serve as messages that sound has arrived.

TO BRAIN

HAIR CELLS

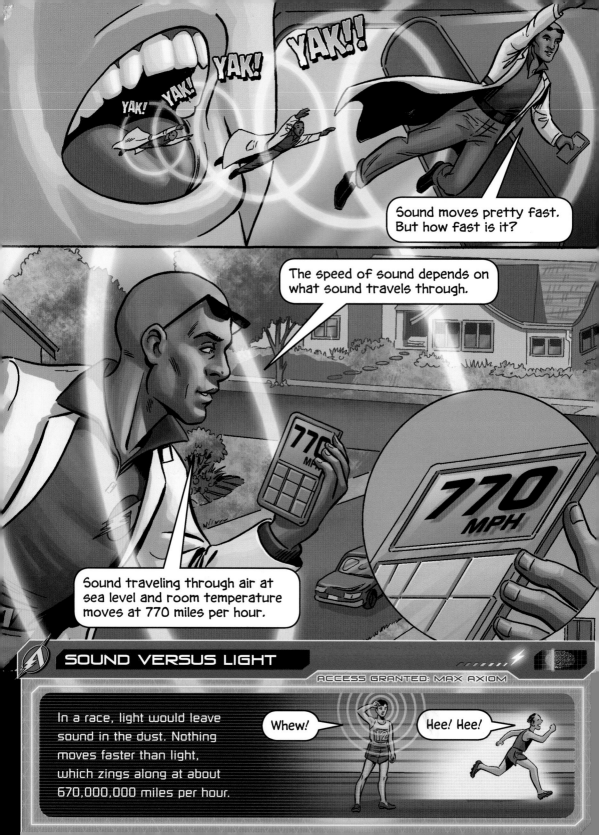

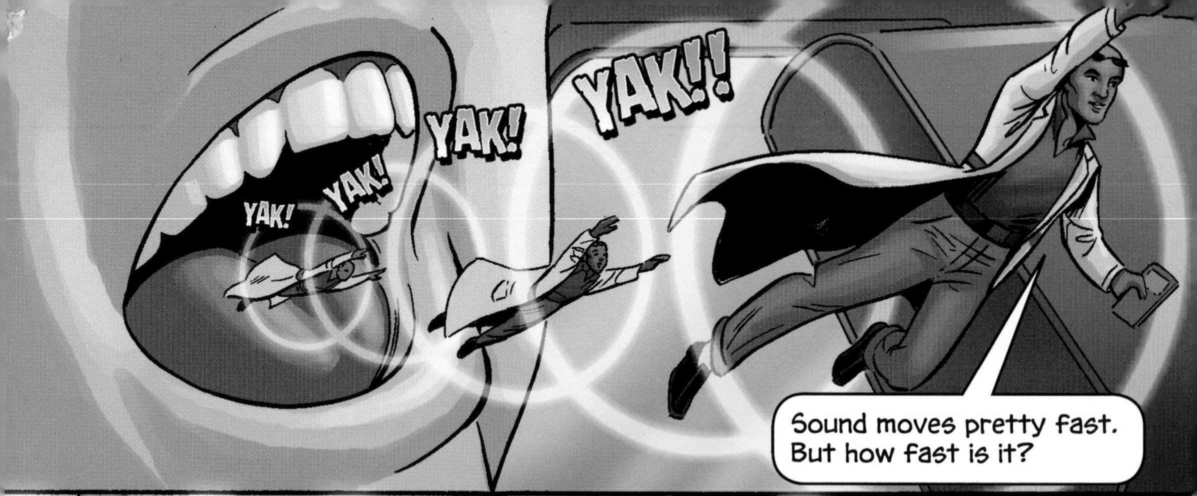
YAK!
YAK!
YAK!
YAK!!
Sound moves pretty fast. But how fast is it?

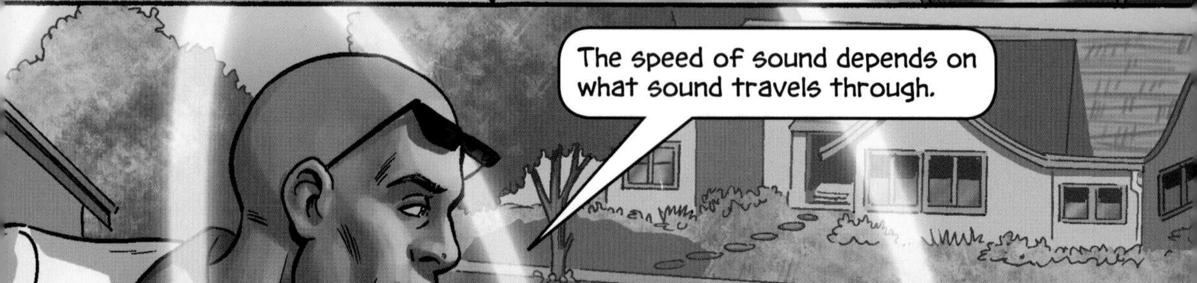
The speed of sound depends on what sound travels through.
770 MPH
770 MPH
Sound traveling through air at sea level and room temperature moves at 770 miles per hour.

SOUND VERSUS LIGHT

ACCESS GRANTED: MAX AXIOM

In a race, light would leave sound in the dust. Nothing moves faster than light, which zings along at about 670,000,000 miles per hour.

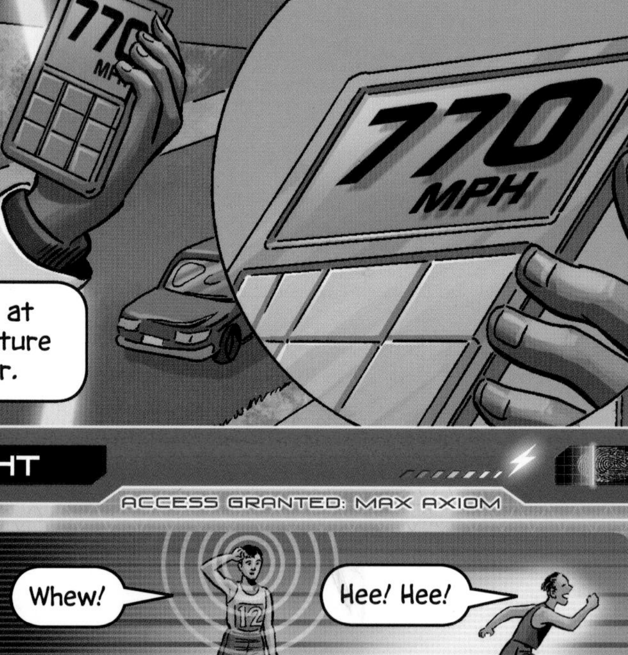
Whew!
12
Hee! Hee!

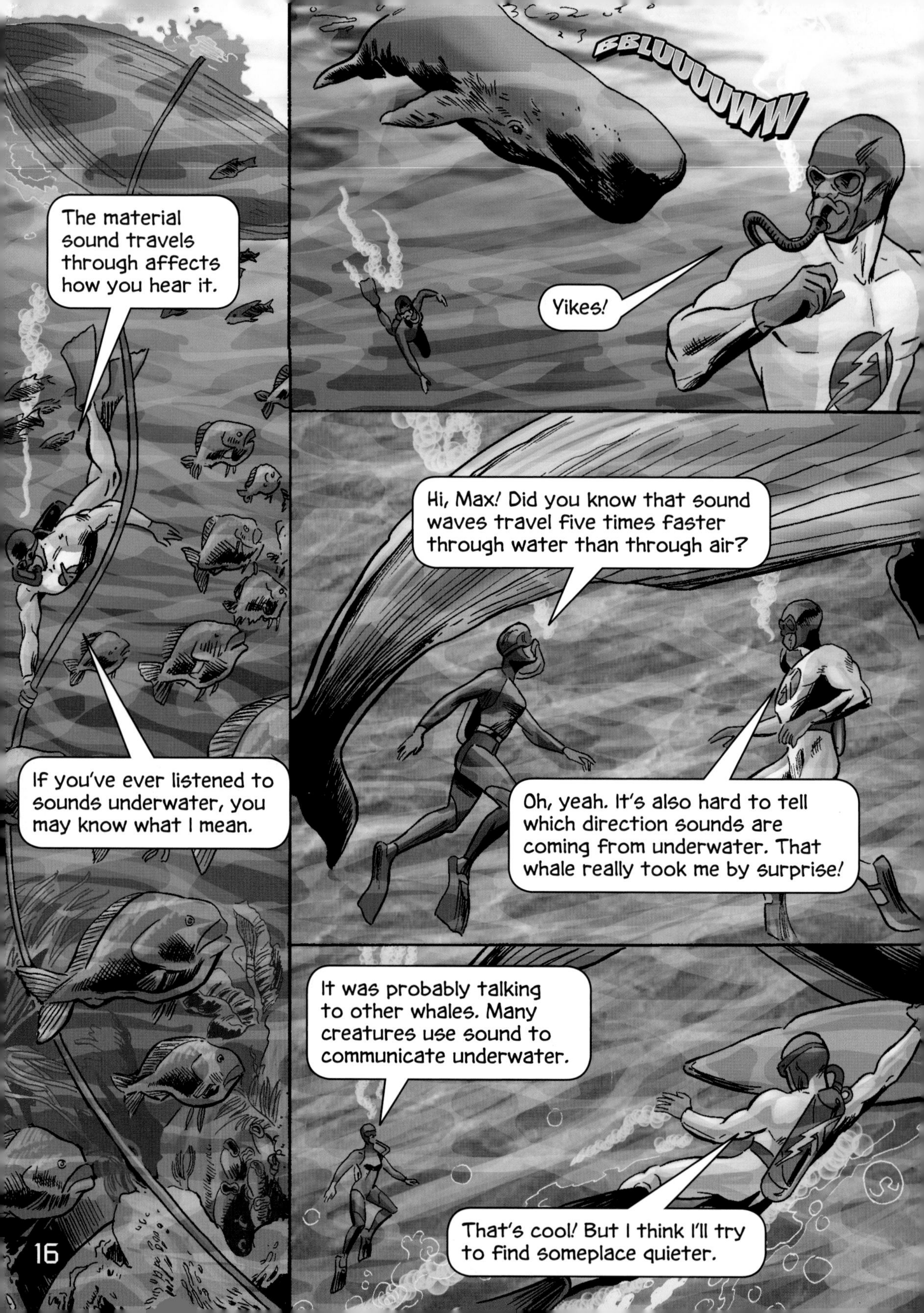

The material sound travels through affects how you hear it.
If you've ever listened to sounds underwater, you may know what I mean.
BBLUUUUUWW
Yikes!
Hi, Max! Did you know that sound waves travel five times faster through water than through air?
Oh, yeah. It's also hard to tell which direction sounds are coming from underwater. That whale really took me by surprise!
It was probably talking to other whales. Many creatures use sound to communicate underwater.
That's cool! But I think I'll try to find someplace quieter.

SECTION 3 WHAT SOUND CAN DO

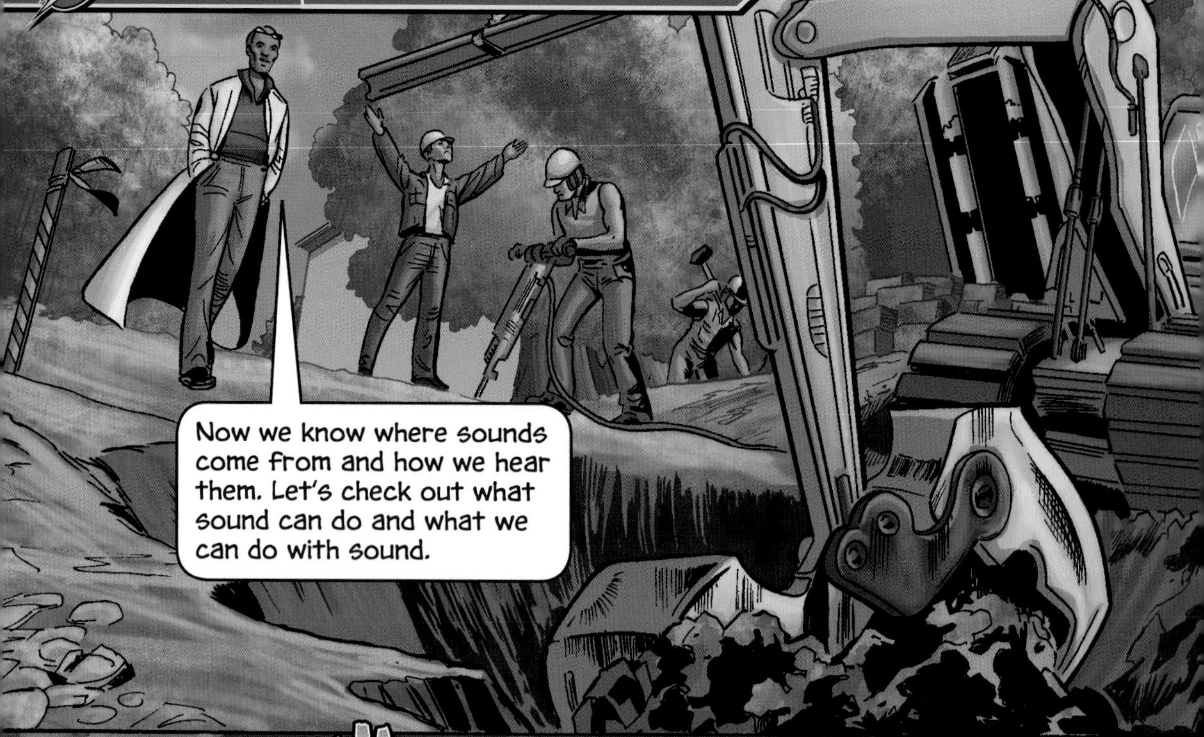
Now we know where sounds come from and how we hear them. Let's check out what sound can do and what we can do with sound.

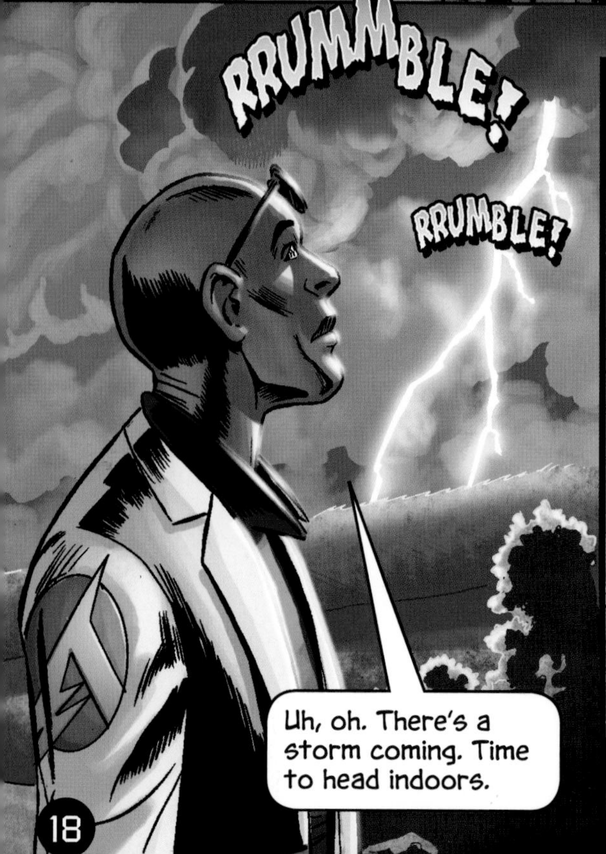
RRUMMBLE!
RRUMBLE!
Uh, oh. There's a storm coming. Time to head indoors.

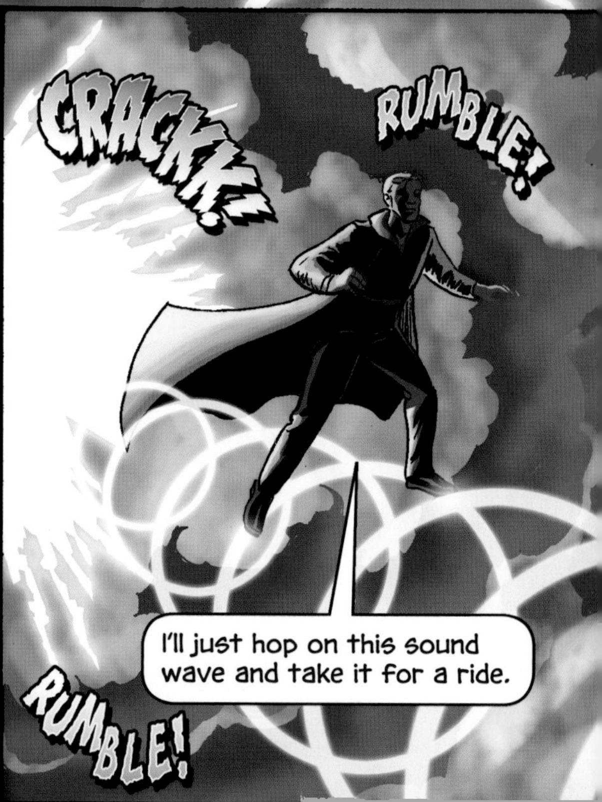
CRACKK!
RUMBLE!
I'll just hop on this sound wave and take it for a ride.
RUMBLE!

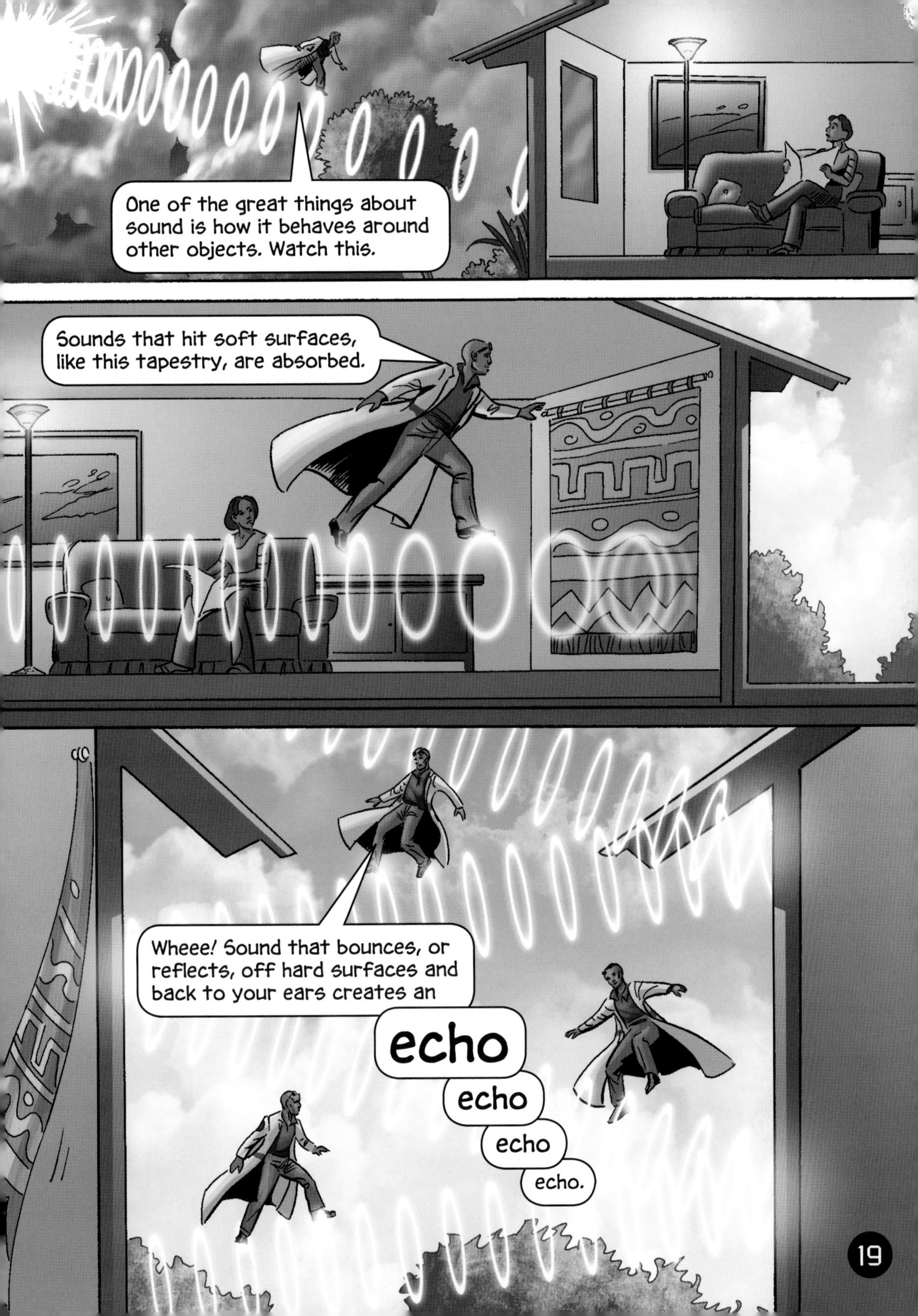
One of the great things about sound is how it behaves around other objects. Watch this.
Sounds that hit soft surfaces, like this tapestry, are absorbed.
Wheee! Sound that bounces, or reflects, off hard surfaces and back to your ears creates an
echo
echo
echo
echo.

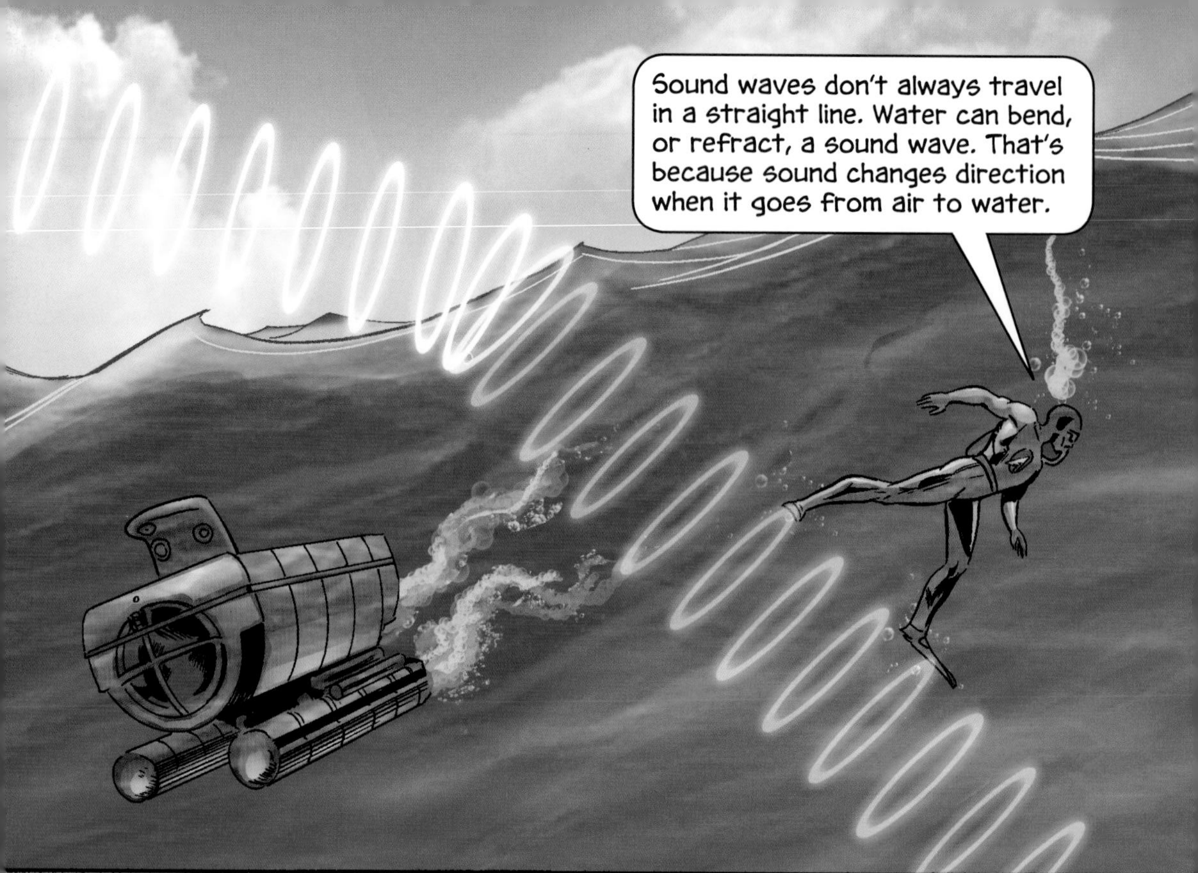
Sound waves don't always travel in a straight line. Water can bend, or refract, a sound wave. That's because sound changes direction when it goes from air to water.

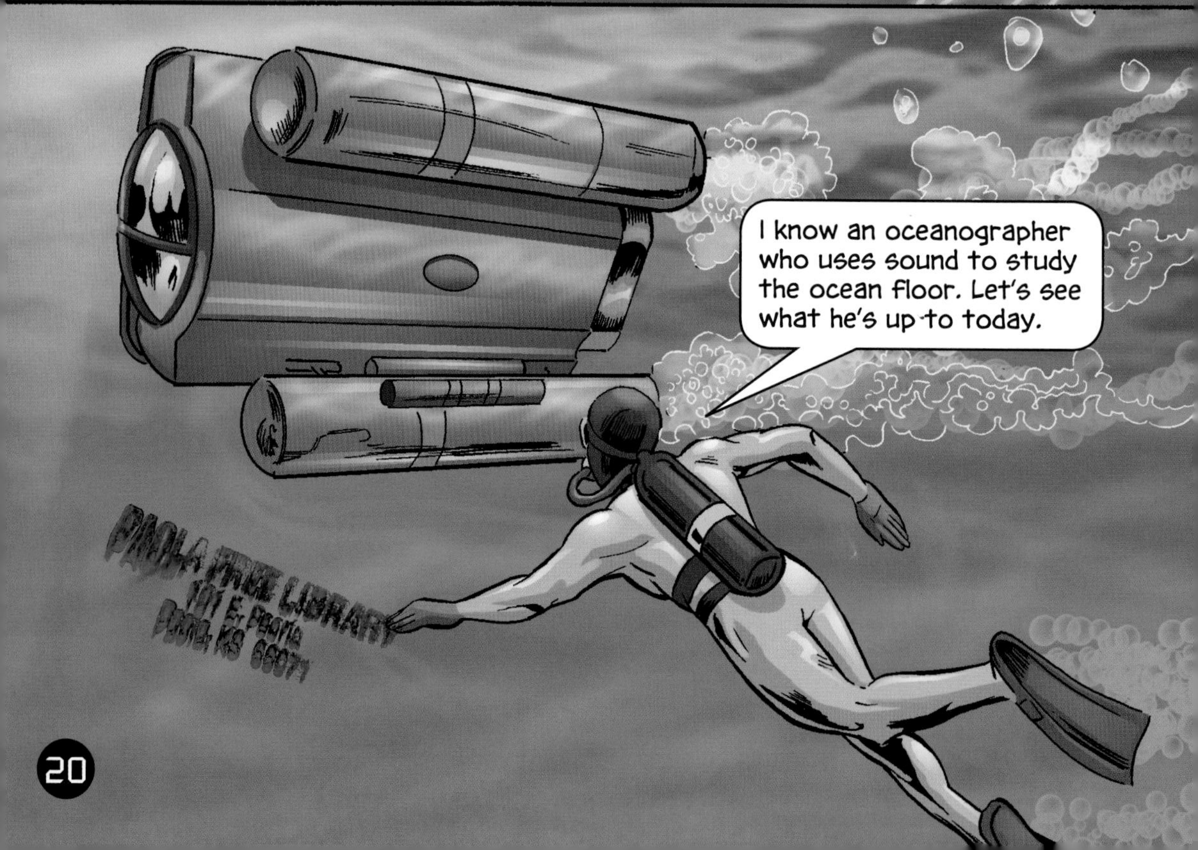
I know an oceanographer who uses sound to study the ocean floor. Let's see what he's up to today.

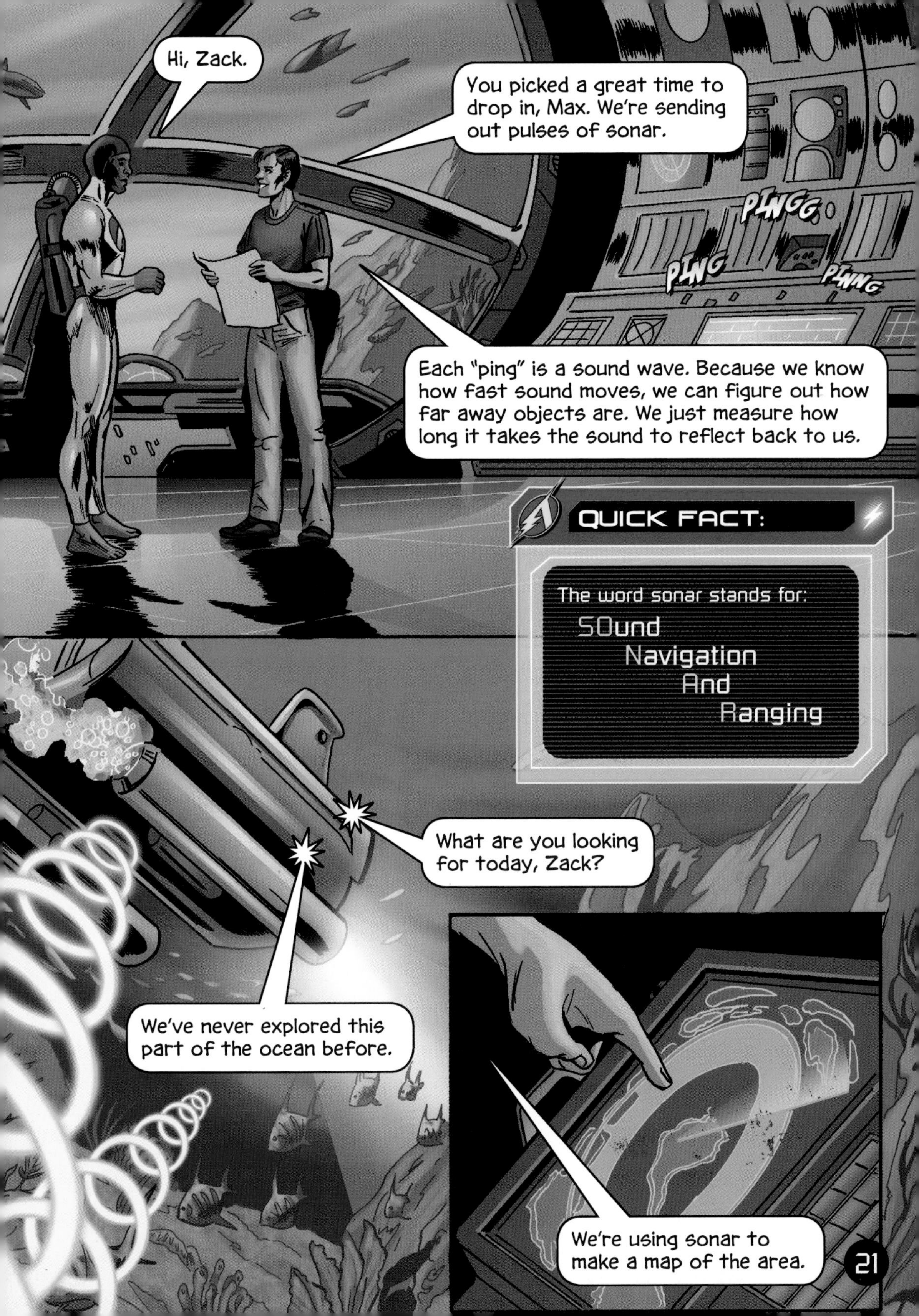
Hi, Zack.
You picked a great time to drop in, Max. We're sending out pulses of sonar.
PINGG
PING
PINNG
Each "ping" is a sound wave. Because we know how fast sound moves, we can figure out how far away objects are. We just measure how long it takes the sound to reflect back to us.
QUICK FACT:
The word sonar stands for:
SOund
Navigation
And
Ranging
What are you looking for today, Zack?
We've never explored this part of the ocean before.
We're using sonar to make a map of the area.

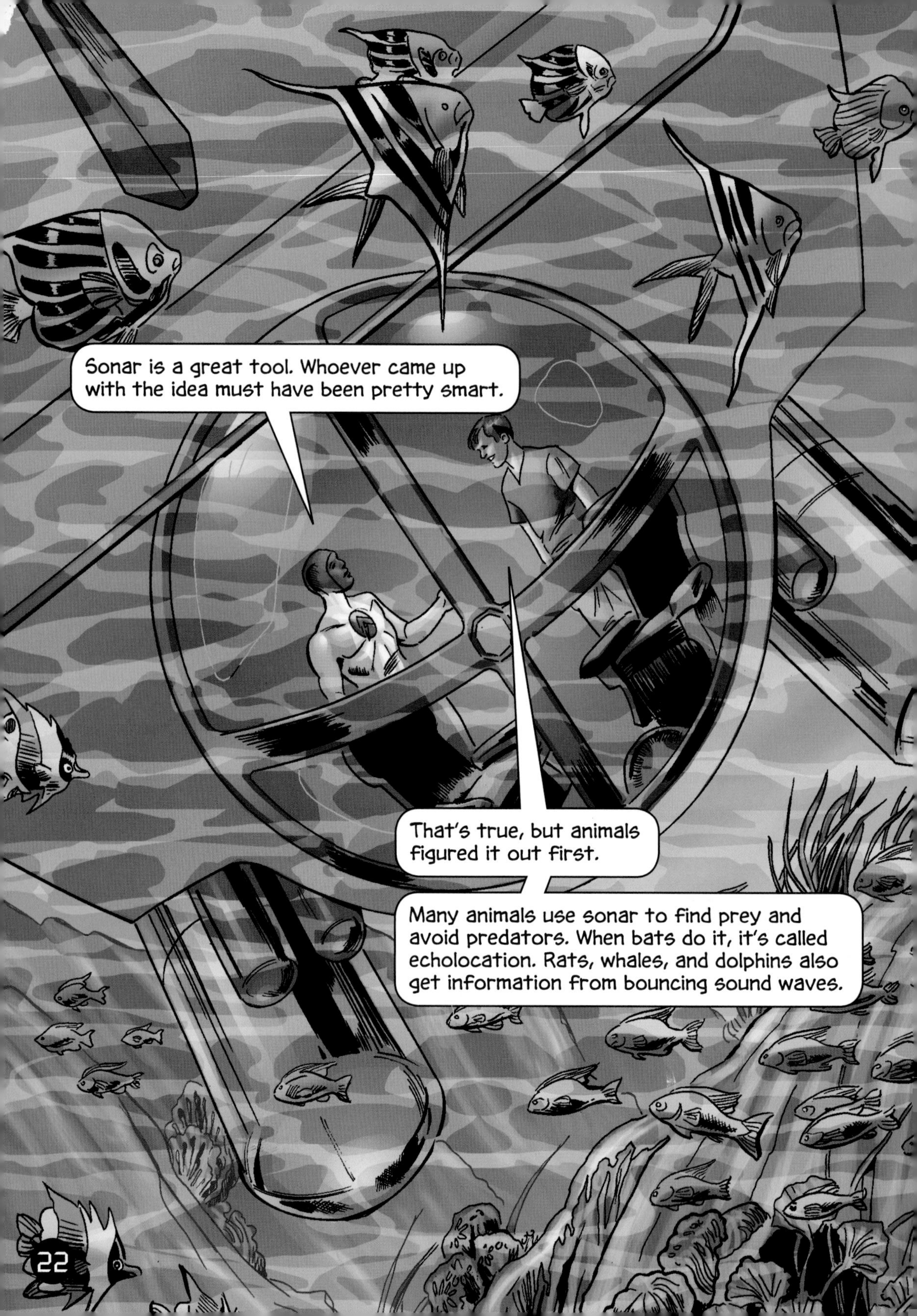
Sonar is a great tool. Whoever came up with the idea must have been pretty smart.
That's true, but animals figured it out first.
Many animals use sonar to find prey and avoid predators. When bats do it, it's called echolocation. Rats, whales, and dolphins also get information from bouncing sound waves.

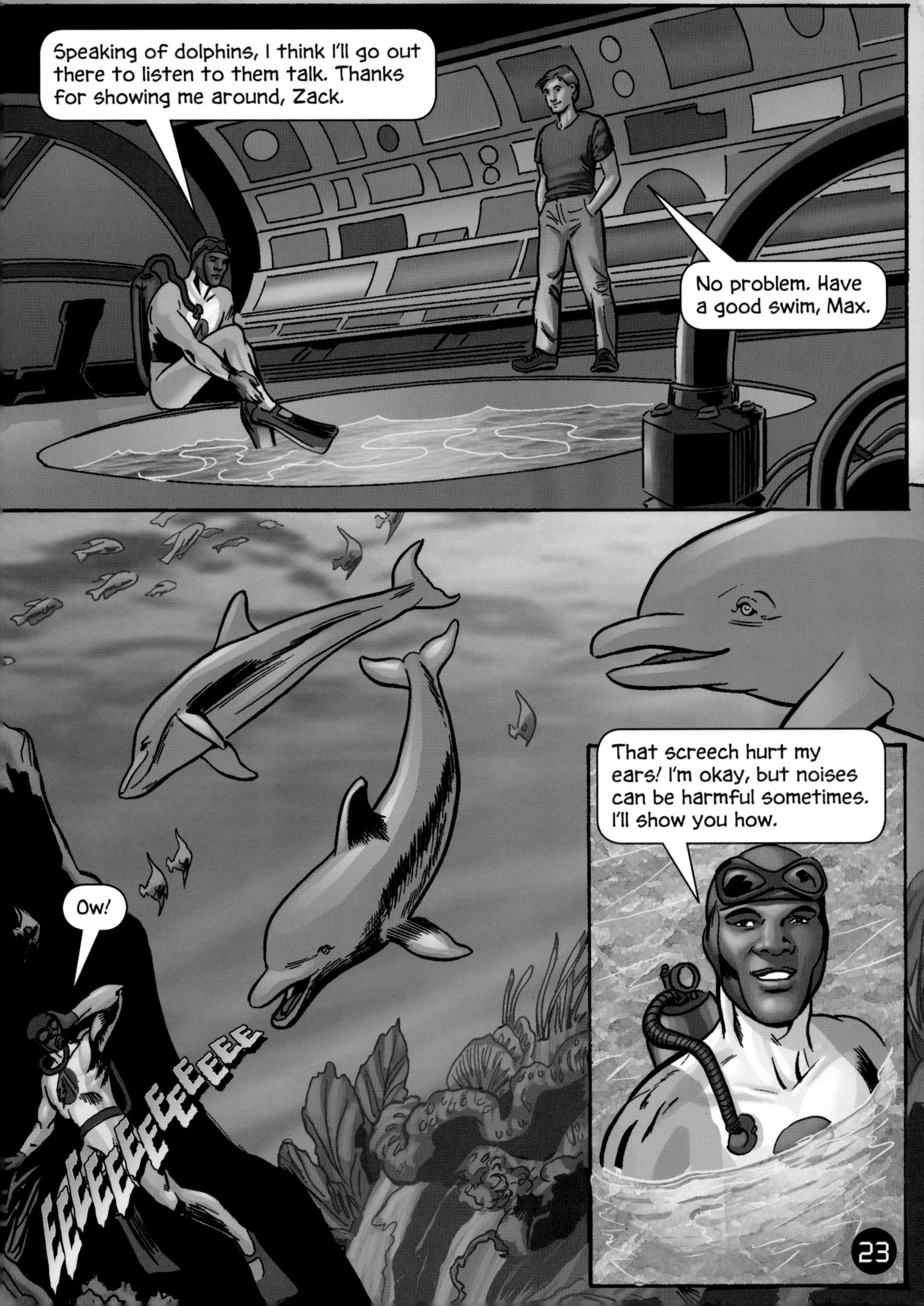

Speaking of dolphins, I think I'll go out there to listen to them talk. Thanks for showing me around, Zack.
No problem. Have a good swim, Max.
Ow!
EEEEEEEEEEEEE
That screech hurt my ears! I'm okay, but noises can be harmful sometimes. I'll show you how.

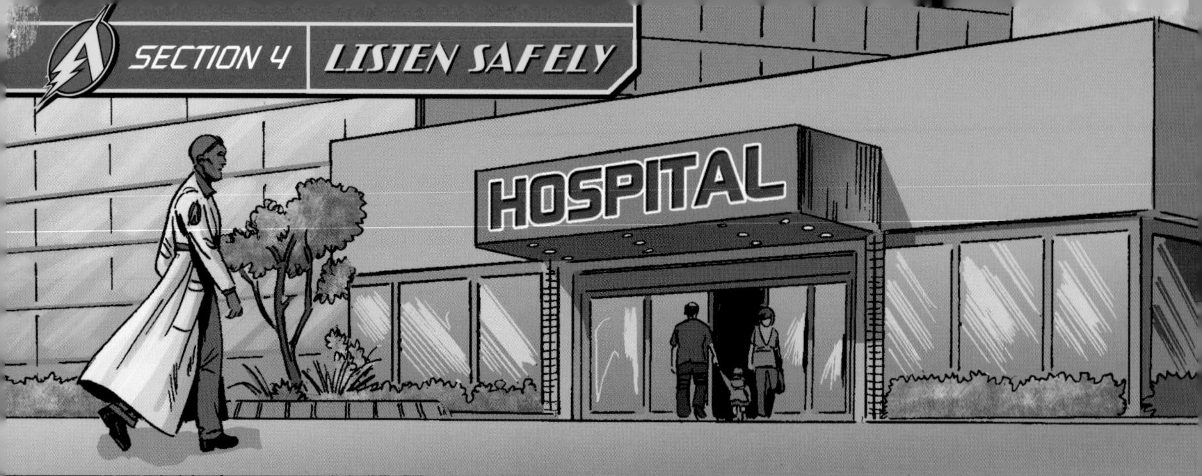
HOSPITAL

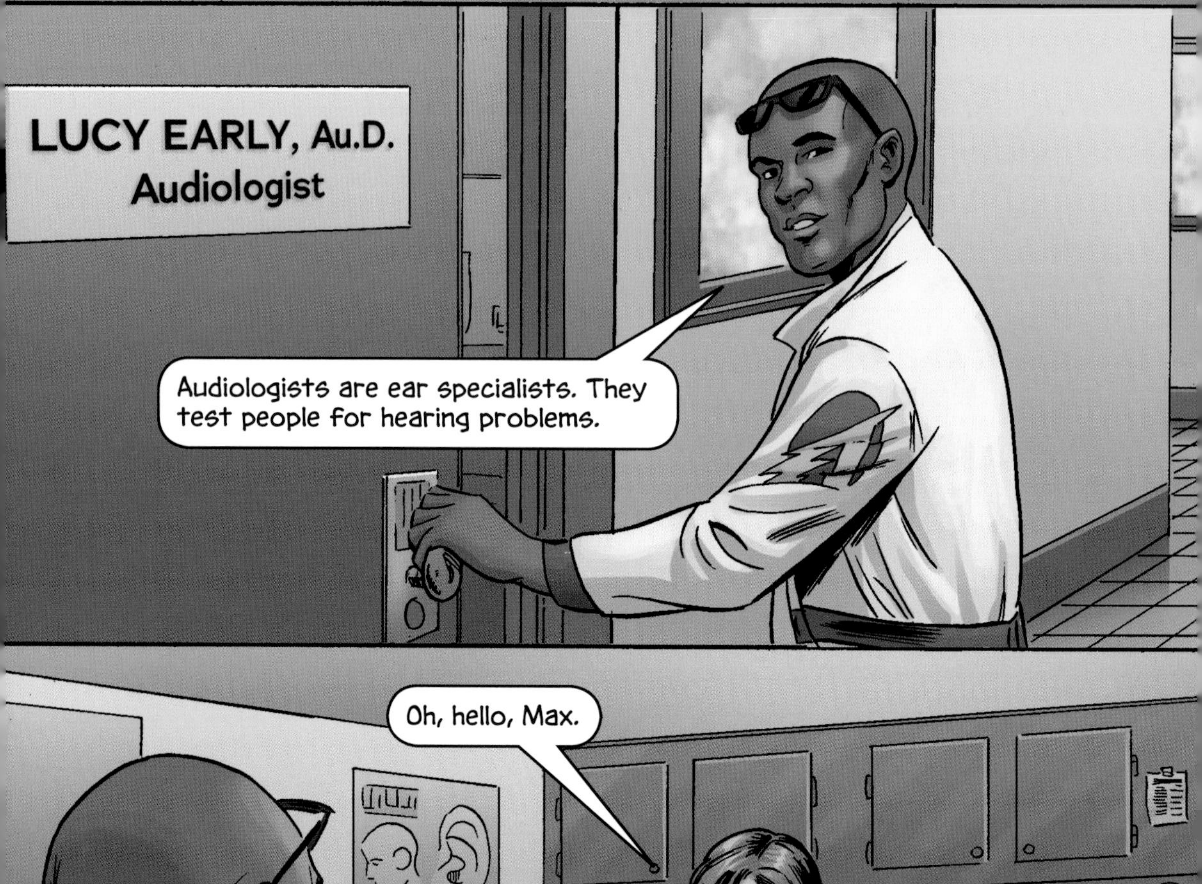
LUCY EARLY, Au.D.
Audiologist
Audiologists are ear specialists. They test people for hearing problems.

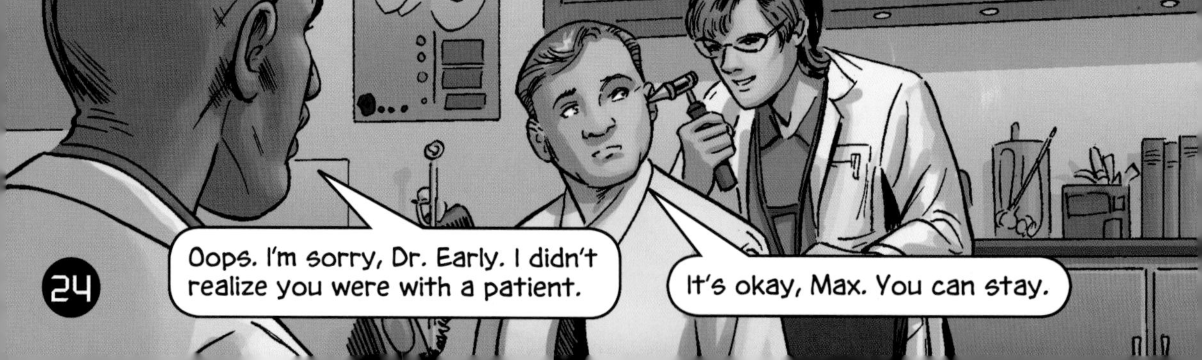
Oh, hello, Max.
Oops. I'm sorry, Dr. Early. I didn't realize you were with a patient.
It's okay, Max. You can stay.

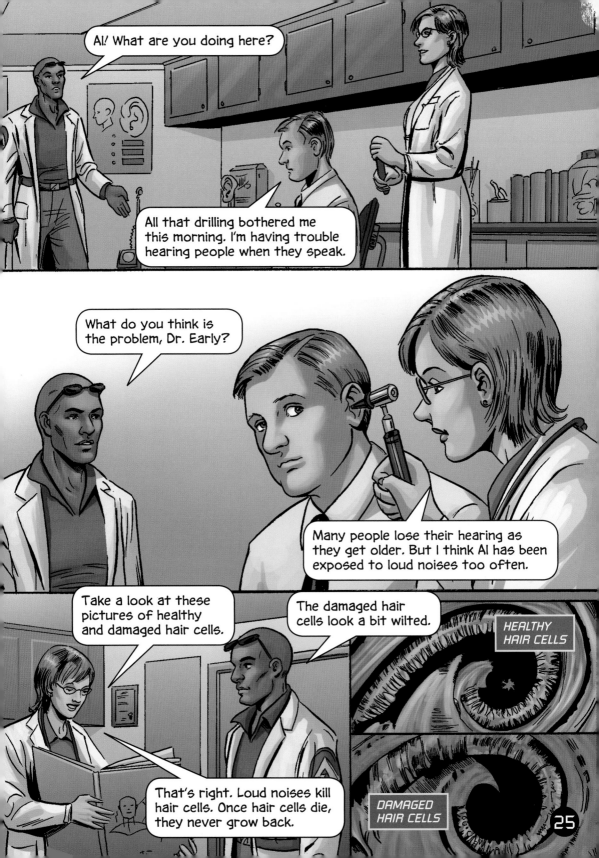

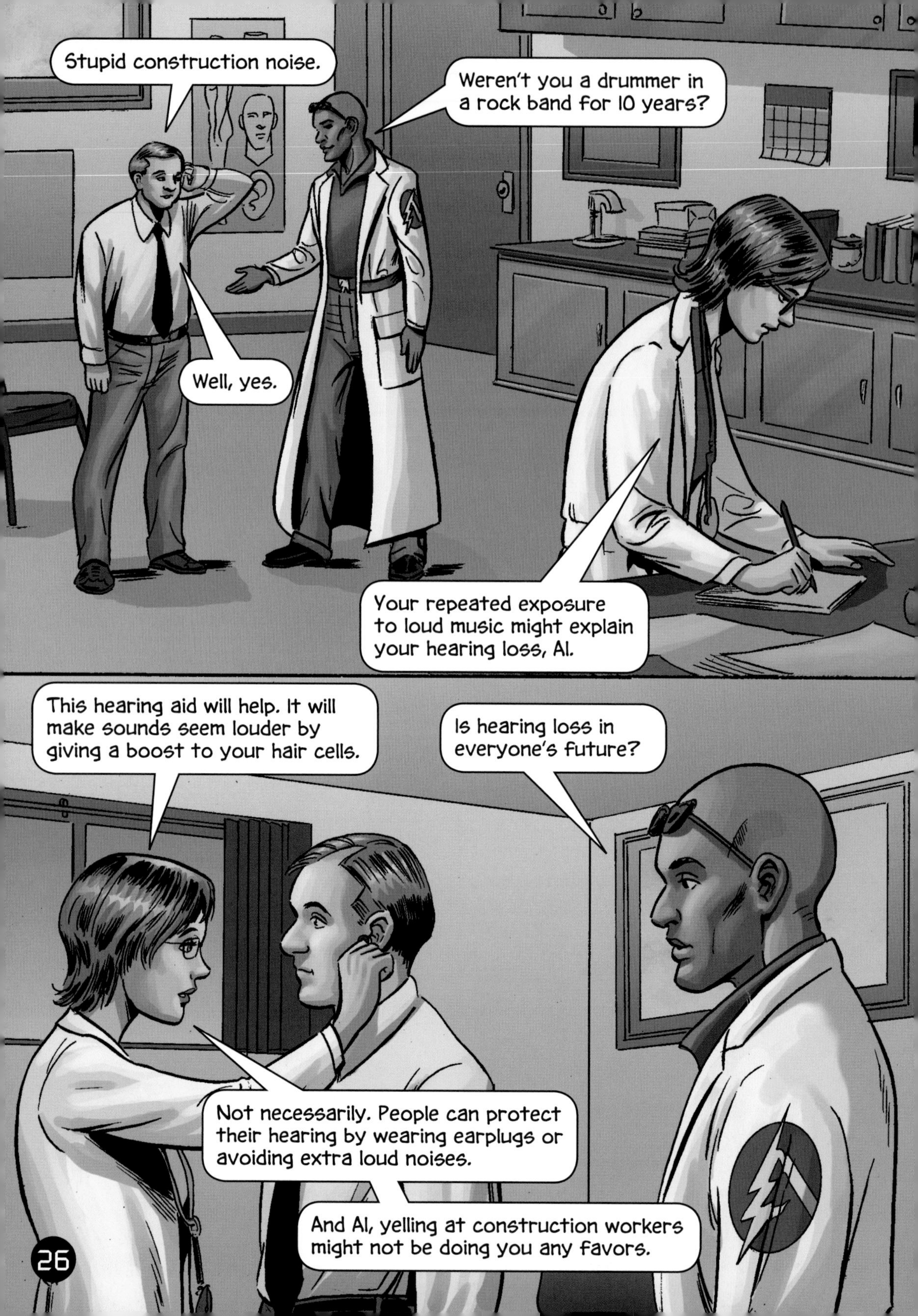

Stupid construction noise.
Weren't you a drummer in a rock band for 10 years?
Well, yes.
Your repeated exposure to loud music might explain your hearing loss, Al.
This hearing aid will help. It will make sounds seem louder by giving a boost to your hair cells.
Is hearing loss in everyone's future?
Not necessarily. People can protect their hearing by wearing earplugs or avoiding extra loud noises.
And Al, yelling at construction workers might not be doing you any favors.

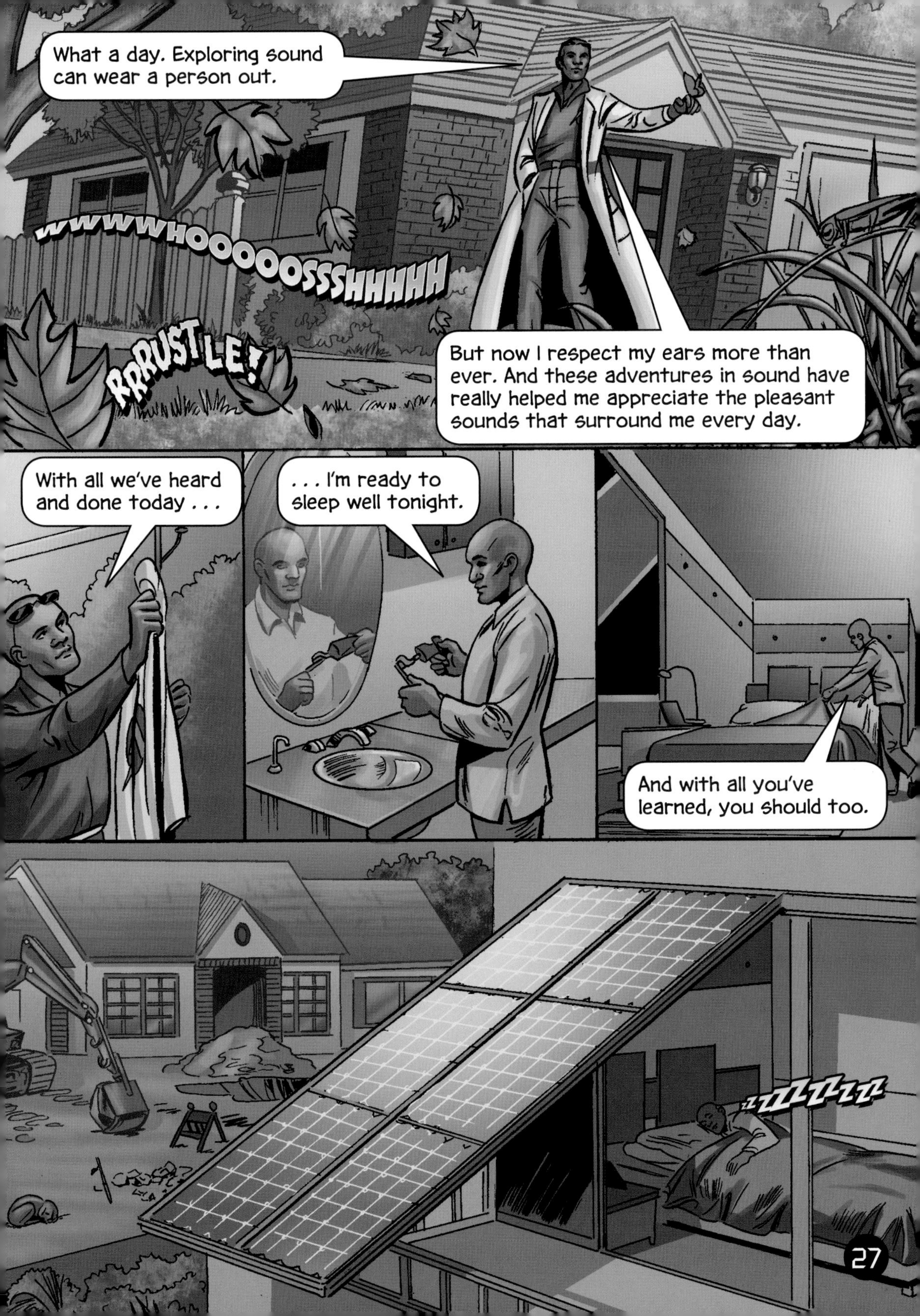
What a day. Exploring sound can wear a person out.
WWWWHOOOOOOSSSHHHHH
RRRUSTLE!
But now I respect my ears more than ever. And these adventures in sound have really helped me appreciate the pleasant sounds that surround me every day.
With all we've heard and done today . . .
. . . I'm ready to sleep well tonight.
And with all you've learned, you should too.
ZZZZZZZZZ

MORE ABOUT SOUND

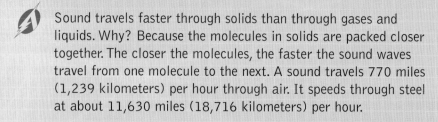

Sound travels faster through solids than through gases and liquids. Why? Because the molecules in solids are packed closer together. The closer the molecules, the faster the sound waves travel from one molecule to the next. A sound travels 770 miles (1,239 kilometers) per hour through air. It speeds through steel at about 11,630 miles (18,716 kilometers) per hour.

Most bats use echolocation to hunt. As they fly, bats release high-pitched sounds that bounce off objects all around them. Based on the echoes they hear, the bats can locate and determine the size of insects fluttering nearby.

The hammer, anvil, and stirrup are the smallest bones in the human body. They are the same size now as they were the day you were born. All together, they could fit on a penny.

Ear wax helps keep your ears clean. As wax forms inside the ear canal, it clings to dirt particles. Eventually, the wax works its way out of the ear, carrying the dirt along with it.

The liquid in the cochlea does more than just magnify vibrations. It also plays a role in balance and helps your body know what is up and what is down.

Elephants use infrasound, or sound below the range of human hearing, to talk to each other. They can use rumbling sounds as low as 5 Hz to communicate.

A cricket's hearing organs are located just below the knees of its front legs. A cicada's hearing organ is on its abdomen.

 Scientists measure the loudness, or volume, of sounds in decibels (dB). A whisper measures about 20 dB, while normal talking is 60 dB. A jet measures about 120 dB and a firecracker exploding is about 140 dB. Any sound above 85 dB can cause hearing damage if listened to for too long. At close range, noise levels above 140 dB cause immediate hearing damage.

 Blue whales are the loudest animals on earth. Their calls have measured 188 dB and can be heard from hundreds of miles away.

MORE ABOUT

SUPER SCIENTIST

Real name: **Maxwell J. Axiom**
Hometown: **Seattle, Washington**
Height: **6' 1"**   Weight: **192 lbs**
Eyes: **Brown**   Hair: **None**

Super capabilities: Super intelligence; able to shrink to the size of an atom; sunglasses give x-ray vision; lab coat allows for travel through time and space.

Origin: Since birth, Max Axiom seemed destined for greatness. His mother, a marine biologist, taught her son about the mysteries of the sea. His father, a nuclear physicist and volunteer park ranger, schooled Max on the wonders of earth and sky.

One day on a wilderness hike, a megacharged lightning bolt struck Max with blinding fury. When he awoke, Max discovered a newfound energy and set out to learn as much about science as possible. He traveled the globe earning degrees in every aspect of the field. Upon his return, he was ready to share his knowledge and new identity with the world. He had become Max Axiom, Super Scientist.

GLOSSARY

absorb (ab-ZORB)—to soak up

cochlea (KOH-klee-uh)—a spiral-shaped part of the ear that helps send sound messages to the brain

decibel (DESS-uh-bel)—a unit for measuring the volume of sounds

eardrum (IHR-druhm)—a thin piece of skin stretched tight like a drum inside the ear; the eardrum vibrates when sound waves strike it.

echolocation (eh-koh-loh-KAY-shuhn)—the process of using sounds and echoes to locate objects; bats use echolocation to find food.

energy (EN-ur-jee)—the ability to do work, such as moving things or giving heat or light

frequency (FREE-kwuhn-see)—the number of sound waves that pass a location in a certain amount of time

hertz (HURTS)—a unit for measuring the frequency of sound wave vibrations; one hertz equals one sound wave per second.

molecule (MOL-uh-kyool)—two or more atoms of the same or different elements that have bonded; a molecule is the smallest part of a compound that can be divided without a chemical change.

pitch (PICH)—the highness or lowness of a sound; low pitches have low frequencies and high pitches have high frequencies.

reflect (ri-FLEKT)—to bounce off an object

refract (ri-FRACT)—to bend when passing through a material at an angle

vibration (vye-BRAY-shuhn)—a fast movement back and forth

READ MORE

Bayrock, Fiona. *Sound: A Question and Answer Book.*
Questions and Answers: Physical Science. Mankato,
Minn.: Capstone Press, 2006.

Cooper, Christopher. *Sound: From Whisper to Rock Band.*
Science Answers. Chicago: Heinemann, 2004.

Dreier, David Louis. *Sound.* Science around Us. Chanhassen,
Minn.: Child's World, 2005.

Parker, Steve. *Making Waves: Sound.* Everyday Science.
Chicago: Heinemann, 2005.

Trumbauer, Lisa. *All about Sound.* Rookie Read-About
Science. New York: Children's Press, 2004.

INTERNET SITES

FactHound offers a safe, fun way to find Internet sites
related to this book. All of the sites on FactHound have been
researched by our staff.

Here's how:
1. Visit *www.facthound.com*
2. Choose your grade level.
3. Type in this book ID **0736868364** for
   age-appropriate sites. You may also browse
   subjects by clicking on letters, or by clicking on
   pictures and words.
4. Click on the **Fetch It** button.

FactHound will fetch the best sites for you!

INDEX